Y0-CFQ-536

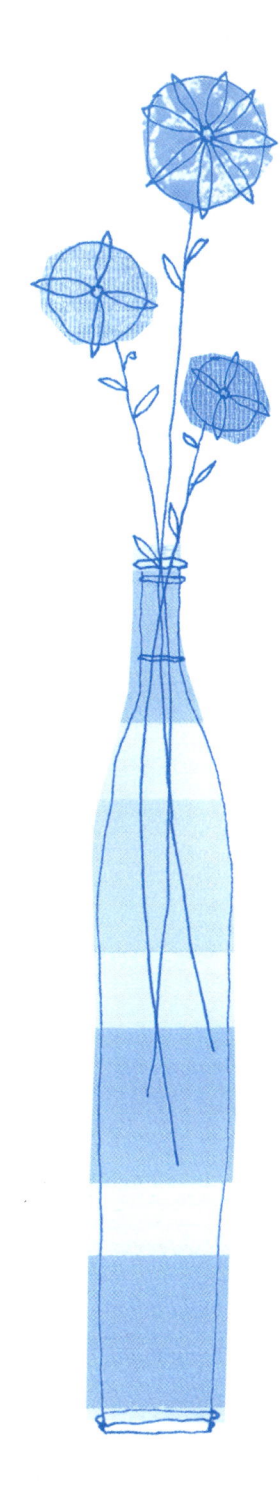

A Gift For:

_____

From:

_____

Copyright © 2012 Hallmark Licensing, LLC

Published by Hallmark Gift Books,
a division of Hallmark Cards, Inc.,
Kansas City, MO 64141
Visit us on the Web at Hallmark.com.

All rights reserved. No part of this publication
may be reproduced, transmitted, or stored
in any form or by any means without the prior
written permission of the publisher.

Editor: Chelsea Fogleman
Art Director: Chris Opheim
Designer: Rob Latimer
Production Designer: Bryan Ring

ISBN: 978-1-59530-517-6
BOK1201

Printed and bound in China

you are BLESSED

Prayers for
Checkout Lines,
Ice Cream, and
Other Simple
Moments

HOLLY MCKISSICK

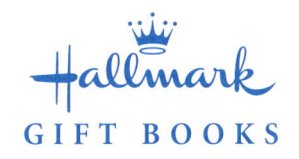

Hallmark
GIFT BOOKS

Table of Contents

INTRODUCTION 1

BLESSINGS FOR RITUALS AND CELEBRATIONS 3

Blessing for My Birthday 5

Blessing for a Loved One's Birthday 6

Blessing for a New Home 7

Irish Wedding Prayer 8

Blessing for My Anniversary 9

Blessing for a New Baby 10

Blessing for Planning a Menu 11

Blessing Before a Meal 12

Blessing for Retirement 13

Blessing for a Garage Sale, Donation, or Spring Cleaning 14

Blessing for Tending a Dying Loved One 15

Blessing for a Funeral 16

The Doxology 17

The Lord's Prayer 18

Blessing for a Family Reunion 19

Blessing for a Party or Celebration 20

BLESSINGS FOR LIFE'S LITTLE MOMENTS 21

Blessing for an Extra Moment Under the Covers 23

Blessing for an Unexpected Gift 24

Blessing for Dusting My Home 25

Blessing for a Leaf 26

Blessing for a Chocolate-Dipped Cone 27

Simple Gifts 28

Blessing for Hard Work 29

Blessing for a Moment of Rebirth 30

Blessing for Exercise 31

Blessing for the Dropped Jar 33

Blessing for Signs of Healing 34

Blessing for Bringing in the Mail 35

Prayer of St. Richard of Chichester 36

BLESSINGS FOR EVERY SEASON 37

Blessing for Any Day 39

Blessing for a Holiday Meal 40

Blessing for Christmas 41

Blessing for Opening a Gift 42

Blessing for the Snow 43

Blessing for the First Bud of Spring 44

Blessing for a Summer Day 45

Blessing for the Harvest 46

Blessing for a Fall Day 47

Blessing for the Rain 48

Blessing for the Sun 49

Blessing for the Moon 50

Blessing for a Difficult Time 51

Blessing for Christ's Presence Every Day 52

BLESSINGS FOR SPECIAL PEOPLE 53

Blessing for the Saints in My Life 55

Blessing for Fathers 56

Blessing for Mothers 57

Blessing for Family Time 58

Blessing for Friendship Through Sadness 59

Blessing for Gadget-Loving Friends 60

Blessing for the Kids in the Backseat 61

Blessing for My Teenager 62

Blessing for Volunteers 63

Blessing for the Friend Who Brings Dinner 64

Blessing for the Mammogram Technician 65

Blessing for the Realtor, Saleswoman, Accountant, and Other Guides 66

Blessing for a New Adventure 67

Benediction for a Gathering of Loved Ones 68

BLESSINGS FOR THE PLACES I GO 69

Blessing for My Home 71

Blessing for My Job 72

Blessing for a Friend's House...73

Blessing for Our Church..75

Blessing for the Farmer's Market 76

Blessing for the Checkout Line 77

Blessing for the Grocery Store..78

Blessing for a World Needing Peace...79

Blessing for Leaving a Place 80

BLESSINGS FOR THE ONE AND ONLY ME 81

Prayer of St. Francis..83

Blessing for Using My Unique Gifts 84

Blessing for Life's Abundance 85

Blessing for a Relationship with God 87

Blessing for the One and Only Me 89

Blessing for Rest and Relaxation 90

Blessing for Generous Living 91

Blessing to Hear God's Call 92

Blessing for My Recovery..93

Blessing for My Hands 94

Blessing for My Limitations 95

Blessing for All of Who I Am..96

*I*NTRODUCTION

A blessing is not something you "deserve" or something you earn. A blessing is a gift, like a perfectly ripe peach or a warm, sunny day in the middle of January. You can't engineer it, can't explain it.

Some of the most familiar blessings come at the beginning of the Sermon on the Mount. Before the challenging instructions to love your enemy, turn the other cheek, and forgive seventy times seventy, the blessings are announced. Blessed are the poor, blessed are the meek, blessed are the peacemakers . . .

If the blessings were only intended for the exceptional Mother-Teresa types, those who have made it over a high hurdle of righteousness, then they would come at the end of the sermon, as rewards for those who have met the requirements. The words would say, "If you have done all these things, kept my commandments, followed my instructions, then blessed are you."

But the blessings come before our striving, before we get to the starting line, before we start working, before we pray, tithe, serve in the soup line, or make a casserole for a friend. It's as if you go to class on the first day, before you have done any work at all, and the teacher passes out the report cards. There it is, a big bold letter: A+. This grade goes not just to you but also to the student in front of you, next to you, behind you, and all around: smiley faces at the top of each paper. And the blessings are not given one here, one there, shared with only the gifted, the fortunate, or the faithful. They are shared with everyone.

The blessings are not demands or instructions, but pronouncements and declarations. Scholars call them "performative language." Jesus says, "Blessed are you," and it is so.

This book is about blessing the over-the-top—and, even more, blessing the humdrum. Because our job in this life is to notice the blessings, to be awake, to be attentive to the world around us—with all its richness and color.

Blessings for Rituals and Celebrations

When we say a blessing—over a golden squash or a silver anniversary—we turn a moment into an event. For just a second, if nothing more, we linger over the holiness in what *is*.

There are certain experiences, such as "life cycle events," that are predictably sacred, experiences when we almost expect to be moved and touched. Like a child's graduation. The long ceremony begins—the endless march of black gowns across the stage—girls in high heels, boys in pinched shoes. The principal begins to speak . . . "There never has been a class quite like this one." The names drone on. Your mind flashes back to the first bite of peas, the first step, the fall from the swing set. Hours spent learning to ride a bike. The time you were separated at the mall—twenty-six minutes that felt like three lifetimes. Somehow, in a blink of an eye, that tiny one was taller than you.

The ceremony stands still. Finally, the principal finishes, and you smile at the person next to you, thinking, "Blessed, we are so blessed."

There are other moments, too—plain, ordinary and routine moments—that spill over with holiness. Like helping my daughter pick up the clothes from her floor, working together and quietly making a straight path from the doorway to the closet. There are times that are like no other time—reading under the covers before bedtime or going to coffee with our young adult just home from college.

In Hebrew, the word for sacred is "qadosh," meaning "set apart." To say a prayer over every moment, whether you are cradling a new life at the baptismal font or running through a sprinkler on a hot summer morning, is to acknowledge that your life is sacred, set apart, holy.

When you bless the moment, tiny or grand, your life becomes a ritual of celebration and meaning.

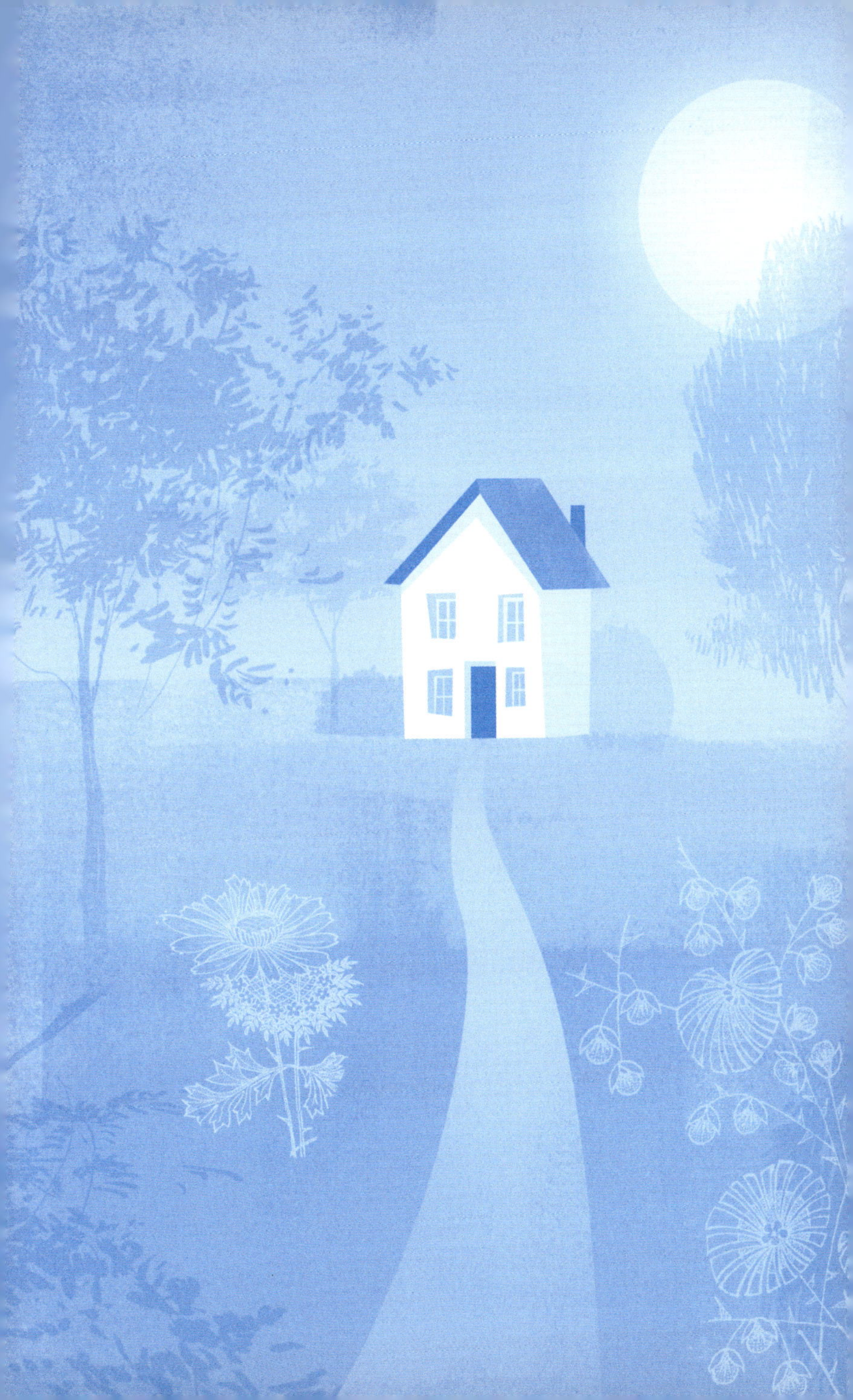

Blessing for My Birthday

For the holy feeling
of "Happy Birthday!" phone calls,
for texts from friends and loved ones,
bless this inexplicably grace-filled day.
For the cards that came in the mail,
today and the day before,
for the gifts and wishes and smiles . . .
For a day when everything inside feels complete
and everything outside feels whole.

Birthday God,
for your creation of which I am a dazzling part,
my soul is full.
May the year that opens before me
be filled with more days
of joy, gratitude, and grace.

Blessing for a Loved One's Birthday

Today is unique.
We sing and bear witness
as a special one blows out
the candles on another year.
We reflect on the past with all that it brought:
new experiences, new friends, new loves.

And we thank You, Sweet One,
for this blessed and transparent moment—
for the opportunity to honor
so much life packed into 52 weeks,
so much gained.
We jump high,
and You carry us higher still.

For this day and the next 365,
blessed are You.

Blessing for a New Home

God, You are my home,
and so You have always been.
You planted me in the garden,
welcomed me onto the ark,
and found a place for me in the inn.
Now I come into a new home.

As I step across the threshold,
may this be a fresh act of creation.
May I leave behind what needs to be left—
uncertainties, regrets, or thoughts
of what might have been.
May I step through the entry
and claim it as a doorway into a life
that is authentic, honest, and open.

May this new home be a vault
to hold my hopes and dreams,
a nest where my longings, full-fledged, take flight,
a retreat where my body is renewed
for the mission of the next day.

Infused with Your Spirit,
may this home be a haven of peace
and a sanctuary of light for all who enter.

Irish Wedding Prayer

May the road rise to meet you.
May the wind be always at your back.
May the warm rays of sun fall upon your home,
and may the hand of a friend always be near.
May God be with you and bless you;
may you see your children's children.
May you be poor in misfortune,
rich in blessings.
May you know nothing but happiness
from this day forward.

Blessing for My Anniversary

Creator of Love, today we look back on the day
we joined our lives as one—
the vows exchanged
and the excitement in our hearts as we stood
on the brink of our future, hand in hand.

We recall the many days since that one . . .
Days when there was no wine,
and You said, "Trust and drink."
And there was wine, startling and sweet.
Days when there was no bread,
and You said, "Feed one another."
And there was bread, filling and strong.
Days when there was no love,
and You said, "Touch one another."
And there was Your love, extravagant and rich.

Every happiness has meant more
for having this dearest one at our side.
Every trial made us stronger.
Every shared adventure has knit us together.

Thank You for this cherished one,
this lover, soul-friend, and partner.
Thank You for the love You give
that floods our spirits and makes us ever ready
to share ourselves, our lives.
For we know that love is Your greatest gift—
and our greatest gift, too.

Blessing for a New Baby

Sweet Spirit of Life,
You are the mystery at the heart of creation.
You set the stars in the sky,
formed the seas and all that fill them.

You fashioned this tiny one, too,
from generous genius and human love.

Blessed are You for all possibility and promise.

By Your guiding Spirit,
may this child's path
be full of kind faces and tender words.
May trials and lessons learned
lead always to a deeper relationship with You.
May this life symbolize the wonders
of Your unending love and inspire us
to build a world where every child
will flourish in Your garden of plenty.

Blessing for Planning a Menu

Delicious and Nourishing God,
we look at beautiful pictures of food
and take simple joy in imagining
how the ingredients will come together . . .

Perhaps a butternut squash soup
with pears and a little cream
or a pumpkin bread with chocolate chips and—
the surprise ingredient—
coconut,
to bring the moist "melt in your mouth-ness."

God who fills us with all good things,
who satisfies us, body and soul,
replenishes, restocks, and restores,
thank You.

For Your nurture and comfort—
anticipated, experienced, and remembered,
hear us as we say grace.

Blessing Before a Meal

O God,
bless this food to our use
and us to Your service;
make us grateful for all Your mercies
and mindful of the needs of others.
Amen

Blessing for Retirement

You made the heavens and the earth,
separated the light from the dark
and called it good.

You made us,
the work of our hands, the fruit of our days
and called it good, too.

God who has given us purpose and meaning,
we give You thanks for the gift of work—
for the brown earth to till and serve,
for losing ourselves in the planting
and digging and sweating,
for using our minds to dream new dreams
and imagine possibilities.

Now let us see what we have done.
Let us look at the work of our hands
and recall how You labored for six days
and on the seventh, rested.
Grant us, too, the space to rest—
time to enjoy the fruits of Your creation.

Blessed be the next stretch of the journey.
May it be renewing, relaxing,
and filled with refreshment and rebirth.

Blessing for a Garage Sale, Donation, or Spring Cleaning

Holy God,
the act of clearing out is complicated.
You lighten our spirits
with every sack we carry to the curb.
Like the first disciples who heard Your call
and dropped everything to follow,
we can imagine the sweetness of a journey
with no bag, no suitcase, no wallet—
traveling, unencumbered.
It is a gift to sift, sort, and set aside,
to think of others who could use these things.

But there are other emotions, too, Holy One.
Help us to find the security and strength it takes
to separate our spirits from "things."
Help us empty, cleanse, and clear.

God of all things familiar and old,
give us the confidence to feel we have enough,
to know we are enough.

Blessing for Tending a Dying Loved One

Thank You, God, for the bedside chair,
for the awesome privilege and responsibility
of being present.
We who can take so many things for granted . . .
We see this time for what it is:
a gift carved out of wonder.
A gift that position, place, and fortune
have made possible.

This is a time like no other.
We sit, we wait, we pray.
The world slows to a crawl.
Breaths grow shallow.
Eating, drinking, and speaking fade.
The body is focused on this final task of letting go—
it is work.
It is labor.
Like birth, it is holy and moving.

As with diapering and swaddling,
nursing and feeding,
how holy that we can care for one another now.

Thank You for this blessed, holy time—
sacred and set apart.
Your final act of creation
is our privilege to behold.

Blessing for a Funeral

God who treasures every life,
not a sparrow falls to the ground
that You do not weep for—
and so we know You hold our concerns
in Your great heart.

We come into Your light,
needing assurance and reassurance,
a shelter from the stormy blast.
We see those we love hurting and struggling,
and our minds fill with questions.

We ask for a fort that will protect us,
and You point us to the world beyond.
You put a shovel in one hand
and seeds for planting in the other.

Hear our thanks, even in this time of loss,
for friends and family who love and listen,
and for Your promise, again,
that nothing will ever separate us from Your love.

The Doxology

Praise God, from whom all blessings flow;
Praise God, all creatures here below;
Praise God above, ye Heavenly Host;
Creator, Christ, and Holy Ghost.
Amen

The Lord's Prayer

Our Creator, who art in heaven,
hallowed be Your name.
Your kingdom come.
Your will be done,
on earth as it is in heaven.
Give us this day our daily bread.
And forgive us our sins,
as we forgive those who sin against us.
And lead us not into temptation,
but deliver us from evil.
For Yours is the kingdom,
and the power,
and the glory,
forever.
Amen.

Blessing for a Family Reunion

God of our Foremothers and Forefathers,
thank You for the chance to gather as family.

May the thoughtfulness of those
who planned this reunion
be passed like a quilt
from one generation to another.

Here together, we are mindful
of Your promise, fulfilled.
Like Sarah and Abraham,
we have grown fruitful and multiplied.
For the new babies among us,
who make us smile
and who push our gazes out, up, and ahead.
For those we have lost,
who we feel among us still
and who now glimpse into Your glory,
hear our thanks.

God of cousins and kin,
may this gathering
deepen our connections to one another—
and our commitment to creating
a world where everyone
is known as brother and sister.

Blessing for a Party or Celebration

Sweet Spirit of Love,
may the feast of family and friends
sharing a laugh over a joke,
a tear over an oft-repeated story,
open our eyes and our hearts
to the feast of every gathering,
simple or grand.
May the hope and delight we have felt
in these moments together
keep tenderness in our words
and gentleness in our touch
forever.

Blessings for Life's Little Moments

We are out of practice when it comes to noticing the earth around us. The average person who visits the Grand Canyon spends two minutes looking at the canyon and forty-five minutes in the gift shop.

Our lives are so frantic that we get a little rusty from the wear and tear we take; some days we would have to fall into the canyon to notice it. So much more for the little moments we pass by every day: the whistle of the wind, the robin at the window, or the greeting from a neighbor.

If you want to love this life—a life that is increasingly complicated and crowded—without changing the channel every time a disaster strikes, then you have to carve out some time to love the simple, to savor the ordinary. To relish those simple things, whatever they are for you—maybe they're the way sunlight feels through a car window or the way your dad clips out college football articles and sends them in the mail.

Blessing the day, and the world, is one part habit, one part art, and one part skill. Once you get started saying grace over the little moments—the clap of thunder, the card from a friend, the sweet taste of squash—it becomes a way of life, a pattern of existence.

If you can find ways to turn the little moments into occasions for wonder and awe, over time, your life—like the grandest of canyons—will be carved out and filled with color.

Blessing for an Extra Moment Under the Covers

Blessed is the peace of early morning light,
the under-the-covers quiet
while I lay still in bed.

God of the Still Peace,
for this time between sleeping and waking,
with my body at rest,
my tensions gone,
tiredness, too . . .

During these few moments
in the quiet dark,
let me feel Your sheltering acceptance
and soul-deep care
from toe to crown.

This is, indeed,
Your holy, hallowed day,
another to rejoice and be glad.

Blessing for an Unexpected Gift

You surprise me, again,
with sights that dazzle and leave me speechless,
with gifts that awaken me to Your presence
when I'm not paying attention.

Like a pink rose outside my window
on a cold November day . . .
beautiful in any season—
but a sight that means even more
when roses should not be in bloom.

Or a gentle conversation
between pediatrician and child—
I don't know whether to laugh or tear up
at the precocious question and tender story.

For every gift, unexpected,
and for all that is beyond description,
my heart is full.

Blessing for Dusting My Home

As I tend to my small corner of the world,
dusting furniture,
I say grace, Holy One, for this moment,
which feels full and complete.
Let me notice the details:
the soft cloth,
the scent of lemon,
the simple movement of a hand
against the grain of wood.

Thank You for the feeling of satisfaction,
for nothing in particular . . .
for a full heart during what should be an unnotable moment.
In you, Dear God, I'm reminded
that all things are clean and possible again.

Blessing for a Leaf

In every leaf, O God, You offer yourself to us.
With every sunrise,
we are invited into the warmth of Your presence.
With every apple,
we taste Your fresh love for us.

For all that moves and lives and breathes,
hear our thanks.
For this earthen home,
so securely and delightfully wrapped around us,
we come with gratitude in our hearts.

For the simple ways You are present to us this day—
in the gift of refreshing rain,
in the crossing guard who waves to us,
in the store greeter who hands us a coupon,
in voices joined in a laugh, a whistle,
a song, a prayer . . .
Hear our thanks,
God of this good day.

Blessing for a Chocolate-Dipped Cone

Sweet God,
thank You for all in life
that is good to the last lick.

For the familiar pattern of the swirl.
For the tiny loop that appears as the cone
is pulled from the machine.
For the chocolate shell and lush cream.
For the crunch of cone.

God of sweet treats and simple pleasures,
You remind us of all that is perfect
for its simplicity and delightfulness.

Simple Gifts

'Tis a gift to be simple,
'Tis a gift to be free,
'Tis a gift to come down where we ought to be,
And when we find ourselves in the place just right,
'Twill be in the valley of love and delight.
When true simplicity is gained,
To bow and to bend we shan't be ashamed,
To turn, turn will be our delight,
Till by turning, turning we come 'round right.

SHAKER HYMN

Blessing for Hard Work

What wonder, Holy One,
that Your creatures take such joy
in a job well done!

How gracious that we feel such satisfaction
when the leaves are raked and bagged,
the lights are on in the house,
the pie comes out of the oven.
When we stand on a ladder,
brushing paint back and forth, oh, so carefully.

For the inspiration we take, too,
in watching others so hard at work—
the teenager bent over the term paper,
the clerk stocking the grocery shelf . . .
Let these be merciful reminders
that You have made us
just a little lower than the angels.

May every effort, big and small,
open us to the holy creation of this earth
and the privileged role we each can play.

Blessing for a Moment of Rebirth

Blessed is this moment of new life,
the stone rolled away, the women running to tell.

Blessed is this moment,
when we are surprised by hope
long after giving up the possibility.

Blessed are all such moments:
Hearing the doctor say, "I got it all,"
holding the new baby,
seeing the first step,
hearing the first word,
making a good friend, a soul friend, after moving to a new city.

For the touch of warm sun
after the cold tomb, the pink slip,
or the papers served—
for new life when we have seen it,
touched it, felt it, lived it.
May these be the mornings we come to expect,
fresh and new, each and every day.

Blessing for Exercise

Thank You, Holy God, for my body,
this sanctuary for my spirit,
and for this chance now to tend to it.
Thank You for the muscles that bear
my weight and carry me,
for tendons, bones, and ligaments
that weave me into Your creation.

Let me move now,
aware of Your genius
coursing through my veins,
aware of my lungs filling with air.
Carry me like a bird in flight,
who gives no thought to how her wings
will take her from branch to branch.

Thank You for Your blessings
of body, mind, and spirit—
for toning, stretching,
and the time to grow stronger still.

Blessing for the Dropped Jar

God of Sudden Disappointment,
the jar falls from my hand,
and now it is gone.

And yet, You offer me a gift, even here,
in this painful lesson:
Carry less.
Put something down.
Don't juggle so much—
the bag, the purse, the laptop, and charger.
Travel lighter.
Have faith in Your abundance everywhere.

Blessing for Signs of Healing

Hear my thanks,
Blessed Redeemer,
for signs of healing that put my heart to peace.

When we learn of someone's recovery,
when we meet a strong soul
who's been knocked down
and yet stands again,
You restore our faith.
Your refrain of resilience comes
over and over,
symbols all around us
that Your healing never fails.

Thank You, God,
for showing up all the time
in people who embody
Your promise of peace.

Blessing for Bringing in the Mail

God of Good News,
thank You for this blessed part of the day.

Sometimes there is nothing special in the mailbox.
Nothing at all—or nothing worth lingering over.
Nothing, save a company hawking vinyl siding
or a new dentist setting up shop.
Even if that is all,
there is still a slight rush of sweet expectation
created by days when the carrier's gifts
have included a handmade card from a friend,
a holiday greeting, or a picture
of two snaggle-toothed kids.

Who knows what there will be?

God of Good News,
blessed is this daily reminder of possibility.

Prayer of St. Richard of Chichester

Thanks be to thee,
my Lord Jesus Christ,
For all the benefits
thou hast won for me,
For all the pains and insults
thou hast borne for me.
O most merciful Redeemer,
Friend, and Brother,
May I know thee more clearly,
Love thee more dearly,
And follow thee more nearly:
For ever and ever.

Blessings for Every Season

In the scripture, the beginning of wisdom—and joy—is attending to God's creation. When you pay attention, what you find is that while there are inexplicable tragedies like tsunamis and famines, at its core, the world is also amazingly reliable, ordered, and predictable.

Consider the patterns. The sun rises and sets. The day is followed by the night. The seasons come and they go. The seed planted and watered grows into fruit. Babies root around until they find their mother's milk.

When we carefully attend to the seasons, we gain trust and confidence in God's abundance—even in the leanest of days. Last year, I let the Christmas decorations linger through the winter. I kept the twinkling lights on the mantel and staircase through February. It was a harsh winter, and God knows we needed the extra light.

Nothing looked particularly out of place until the end of March, when the crocuses in our yard began to push their way through the frozen earth. Overnight, the holly leaf garland looked wilted and tired.

I took the nativity set down, putting the Baby Jesus in a box and carrying Him out to the garage. Passing the freezer, I thought of the ratatouille I'd made the past summer with vegetables from our garden. I recalled how I'd grown weary of chopping tomatoes, zucchini, and eggplant.

My friend Kris had encouraged me over her stove: "When you make too much, freeze some of it. Then you can pull it out in the dead of winter, and it's the taste of summer."

She was right. On this bitter March day, I dug hopefully through the freezer. There it was, fallen behind the hamburger buns and the Texas pecans: a plastic bag of grace. As I reached my hand for that frozen goodness, I thought of spring and summer and the sure taste of grace to come.

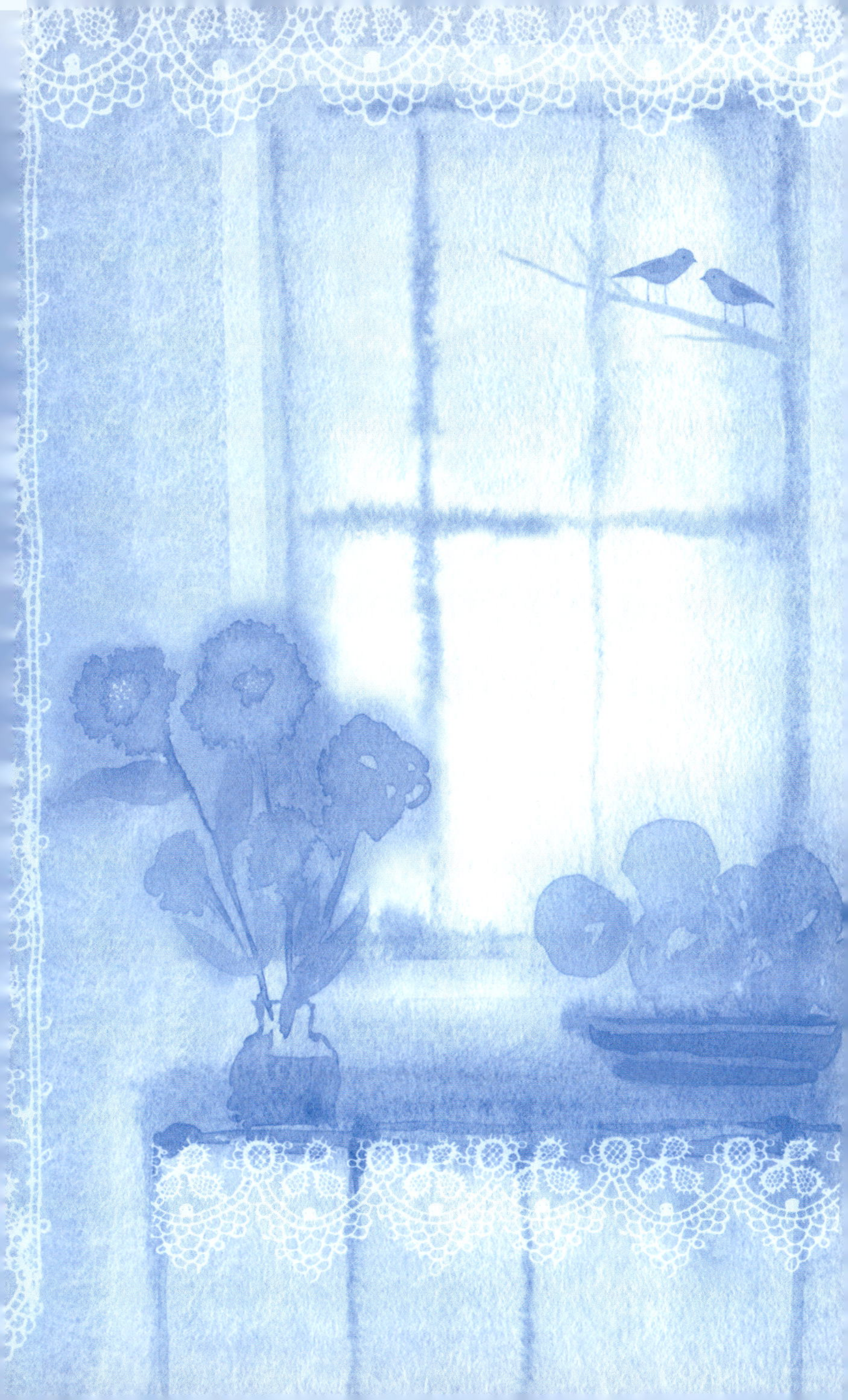

Blessing for Any Day

Your bountiful presence
is the gift of this day and every day.
Where could we go, Dear One,
that You would not already be?
If we make our bed in the depths, You are there.
If we fly to the heavens, there, too, we find You.
Close in front, close behind.
Your right hand holding us,
Your left hand guiding us.

Your bountiful presence is our dearest gift.

Hear our thanks for Your presence.
We feel its generosity
in the first light of morning,
the newspaper on the step,
the smell of coffee, poured and shared,
the sleepy child dressing for school,
the teacher who holds the door and smiles . . .

Your bountiful presence is our deepest gift.

For the birds whose love song is Your song,
for the sun whose warmth is Your warmth,
for the stars whose shimmering light is Your light,
hear our thanks.

Blessing for a Holiday Meal

God of Tradition,
thank You for this feast,
long-anticipated.

We are thankful for everyone here.
Today, much more than carving a turkey,
we have carved out time to be together.

May we see the effort each has put into being here
as part and parcel of the gifts we bring this day.
Hear our thanks, Sweet Spirit of Life,
that You have brought us safely together.

May our table and our talk
remind us of Your presence
in every birth and death,
every joy and sorrow.
May the comfort of each other's company
make us ever more sensitive to those
who are isolated and alone.
Strengthen us, body and soul,
to create a world where Your loving presence
is felt by each one and every one.

Blessing for Christmas

God of the Manger,
give us, please, a role in Your sacred story.
We want to ride on the donkey with Mary
and seek shelter with Joseph.
We want to hear the angels sing
and gaze with the shepherds,
wide-eyed with wonder
under a starlit sky.

In the darkness,
make our paths straight.
Encourage our steps alongside friends
who share our journey.
Warm our hearts as You open the stable door.

Lead us, Merciful Light,
with Your star of wonder—
that all we say
and all we do
might be signs of Your love on earth.

Blessing for Opening a Gift

Holy One,
as I open this parcel,
the giver's generous spirit
comes to me.

No matter the color, size, or pattern of this offering,
I will have received what I need and want.
Even more:
I will have received an invitation
to return a gift of love.
Let me feel the sweetness in this invitation.
Let me hold the giver in my heart.

Gracious, Gift-Giving God,
may we always be
grateful, generous, kind.

Blessing for the Snow

God of the Winter Storm,
how confident You must be
to send a blanket of snow.

Steady us when we step onto the ice.
Remind us, patiently,
to clear the frost from our windshields,
that we might see what is ahead and behind.
Grant us the traction to make our way safely.

God of Winter's Blast, You know we can be
lukewarm in our commitments.
How sure You must be to trust now
that we can make room for those without shelter.

Thaw our spirits,
that we may stay inside
without shutting the world out.
May we know the warmth
that comes from drawing close to You
and wrapping our arms around one another.

Blessing for the First Bud of Spring

God who does not give us an old day,
but a new one, a fresh one,
thank You for the first buds of spring.

For frozen earth that slowly and stubbornly yields,
for the bulb pushing
tenderly, gingerly, persistently up . . .

We never know what will emerge first,
God who makes us look twice—
Will it be the crocus, pale pink by the door,
or the lilac near the walk?
You bless us with mystery and wonder.

We only know what will follow—
more color,
more surprise,
more grace.

Hope, which was planted, buried,
and all but forgotten,
will be resurrected in Your time
and offered to us again.

Blessing for a Summer Day

God of Summer Gifts,
we bask in the glory of blue sky
with a gentle breeze,
in the taste of berries baked in a cobbler,
in the crunch of peanuts at a ballgame,
and in memories of simpler times—
trips to the swimming pool and park.

Thank You for the last day of school,
for little kids squealing as they run,
and teenagers roaring away.
We feel a joyful release of energy in the air.
Thank You, too, for shows in the park
and fireworks at night,
for the bells of an ice-cream truck,
and the songs of locusts, deafeningly loud.

When You designed this
yearly vacation for Your children—
You must have known we'd need the break!
Known how we would treasure it, savor it,
and long for it, year after year.

Blessing for the Harvest

God of the First Garden,
You have filled our lives with bounty,
formed the earth and all that fills it
with Your generous love.
May we be more than attentive this day—
may we be awed and amazed
at the apples that fill our kitchen:
Jonathan, Granny Smith, Rome.

Beneath the shiny skin and sweet fruit,
may we find seeds of justice and hope
in the labor of old men and little ones
who travel from citrus grove to apple orchard
to potato field, harvesting.

Nourished, sustained, and enriched,
may our lives produce Your love
and mercy in abundance.

Blessing for a Fall Day

For leaves the color of firelight
against a blue-sky backdrop,
for the red bush blazing in the yard,
Your holiness breaking in
and marking this earth, this space,
this moment as sacred . . .

For these gifts,
which lift our gazes and spirits,
hear our hearts sing!

Leaves crunch under our steps,
awaking us to Your glory,
reminding us of Your presence everywhere.

Blessing for the Rain

God of the downpour and the refreshing drops,
some days, it comes from the sky
like a much-anticipated guest.
It arrives to work an unseen magic.
Where there was bare dirt,
there will be green shoots,
and in a month, we'll have
grass and flowers and vegetables.

Some days, the rain comes,
and it is out of control.
The creek jumps the bank.
The house and its treasures are lost.

Some days, it is simply too much.
The rain is a sign we must heed:
"Slow down, sweet child.
Slow way, way down.
The streets are slick.
The tires will skid."

Thank You for Your rain,
which covers and floods,
and then, blessedly, mercifully,
recedes and reveals, parting the heavens
with the promise of life abundant.

Blessing for the Sun

Every day, God of Light,
Your sun greets us.

In the winter sky, low, it peeks out.
Outside the wind bites and blusters,
but through windows we feel toasty,
even sleepy, in the afternoon rays.

Thank You for the spring sun,
fresh and new,
moving higher each day in the sky,
thawing Your creation
and beckoning new life from the soil.

Mid-July arrives,
and Your light comes, in full force.
Finally, tomatoes ripen,
the flowers make their last stand.
Children dive into the pool.

In the autumn sky,
Your sun is an impressionist painter,
lighting a canvas
of orange, crimson, and gold.

Every day, Holy One,
the sun feeds, enlivens, and illumines,
telling us there is no moment left unblessed.

Blessing for the Moon

God of Light and Beauty,
You give us this luminous moon,
shining on our sleepy world,
turning our planet into a sparkling blue jewel.

Whether it's waxing or waning,
low or high,
we find the moon there,
hanging deep in the night sky,
and we feel the movement of Your earth.

Holy God,
wake us from sleep to see Your radiance,
and give us the wisdom to recognize
Your light.

Blessing for a Difficult Time

You have promised, Holy One,
that there is nothing in all creation
that can separate us from Your love.
Nothing in height or depth,
nothing present or to come,
nothing in life or death,
nothing in all creation.
Nothing can separate us from Your love.

Even so, difficult times come—
times when we cannot remember
who we are or what we yearn for . . .

Come to us now with Your assurance
that there is no rip You cannot repair,
nothing broken You cannot bind up.
There is no hurt You cannot make whole,
nothing inside of us or outside of us
that can ever separate us from Your love.

Blessing for Christ's Presence Every Day

Christ with me, Christ before me, Christ behind me,
Christ in me, Christ beneath me, Christ above me,
Christ on my right, Christ on my left,
Christ where I lie, Christ where I sit,
Christ where I arise,
Christ in the heart of everyone who thinks of me,
Christ in the mouth of everyone who speaks to me,
Christ in every eye that sees me,
Christ in every ear that hears me.
Salvation is of God.
Salvation is of Christ.
May your salvation, God, be ever with us.

FROM THE LORICA OF SAINT PATRICK

BLESSINGS FOR SPECIAL PEOPLE

When I called the mutual fund company, I was put on hold. It wasn't too unpleasant, thankfully. There was no music and, better, no report of the market's highs and lows.

I was trying to figure out a strategy for my children's college financing maze. The morning had started off with my yearly mammogram. It wasn't just the pink ribbons decorating the office that had reminded me life is fleeting. On the way home from the doctor, I listened to the oldies station, my ears full of songs from times gone by.

Then I arrived home, needing to make this phone call. "Just for security purposes," the woman on the other end asked, "when you were in kindergarten, what was your best friend's name?" It caught me off guard, as did my tears.

"Misty," I said, my voice breaking with all that Misty did—and does—mean to me.

No wonder we call Jesus a "friend." Friends aren't just folks to pass the time with. They keep you alive. They help you face stress and survive cancer. They make the popcorn more buttery and the movie more meaningful. They get in your face and remind you it's not the market that matters but the meaning in every moment.

God shows up, from the first breath to the last, in the special people who share our lives.

Blessing for the Saints in My Life

God of All People,
for those who have gone before us,
for those with us now,
and for those who will shape the future,
our hearts are full with saints living and past . . .
Those who challenge us
to be more than we think possible.
Those who call us to leave the world a better place.
Those who say, "You can do it,"
or "Just do your best."

Hear our thanks, Holy One.
We are grateful for all those saints
who draw on their best—
to draw the best out of us.

Blessing for Fathers

Dear One,
we give thanks for the lines of connection
that bind us to one another.

For fathers who tether us to the earth,
ground us in our sense of self,
and hold us firmly, wildly, strongly.

For fathers who teach us to ride a bike,
to dive off the board, or to drive a car—
the ones who change our oil, slip us a little money,
and always pay for dinner.

Their words of direction
and many acts of love live in our hearts forever.

Bless the fathers and the fatherly,
imperfect and oh, so human,
for their predictable quirks
and dependable patterns,
for their firm and tender love.

Bless their commitment and effort,
and grant us understanding and peace
for all that has been.

Blessing for Mothers

Great Nurturing God,
among Your greatest gifts
are these women who gather us around them . . .
Hens gathering their young,
calling us, and sheltering us in their wings.

Some days we come quickly,
some days slowly.
Always we find them there,
wings outstretched,
bodies warm and reassuring.

Bless our moms and those women
who have mothered us.
Bless those who have been capable
and those who have been less so.

Their gifts are too big to understand.
For the ways they have been capable, superlative—
and occasionally less than perfect—
bless them.
They have made us who we are.

For an inexpressibly soft touch,
an encouraging word,
and loving hearts melted around our own,
thanks be to You, Mothering God.

Blessing for Family Time

Gracious God,
thank You for this time together,
this moment of family unity
when we feel the love
and connection of generations.

We see the gifts You give us
in each other,
and our hearts are full
with gratitude and grace.

Blessing for Friendship Through Sadness

Dear One,
here's a blessing for this sad moment.
Even more so, here's a blessing
for the presence of my forever friend
at a time when loss
sweeps over me.

Bless this caring voice in my ear:
steady, sure, and forever,
a voice that calms my racing heart.
Bless the safety and grace of a friend's heart
in which I can feel pain.
Bless the merciful moments
when we've been the other's rock.

Blessed is this friend who witnesses
and restores me to life.

Blessing for Gadget-Loving Friends

Bless those wonderful souls
with their mixture of talent, knowledge,
and inspiration . . .
They provide us such gifts.

Thank You for those who can connect us
to the world and make our lives
run just a tiny bit more smoothly.
When we see their knowledge at work,
may we sense the hope, healing, and possibility
that are ever present in our lives.

Bless the technique, bless the quirk,
bless the offerings
of our gadget-loving sisters and brothers.
Bless those who guide and connect,
who direct and correct.

For blessed, too, are the moments
when we can lighten our loads
with an intelligent turn of a knob
or punch of a button.

Blessing for the Kids in the Backseat

Blessed are You, Awesome God,
for kids in the backseat.

For the conversation overheard,
whispers and a laugh. . .
For a story shared.
For grins flashing in the rearview mirror.

For the holy fun of growing up
and for the privileged moments
in which we catch a glimpse
of yesterday's child, of the teenager to come,
of the one who will, too soon,
be up and out of the nest.

Bless You now for this chance to listen in.
Bless the stirring of peace and pleasure it brings.

Blessing for My Teenager

Blessed is this young person—
so independent now.
She manages her life,
going from class to extracurriculars,
from friends to family,
all while texting with one hand.

Bless the small things
I can do now.
The simple forms of care
that she will still allow and take.
Let my simple acts of love
mean as much as those that have gone before—
from bathing her little body
to pushing her on the park swing.

Let this young adult,
this pride of my heart,
feel my love now and always.
Blessed are the moments
when I offer a gift,
and she is open to receive.

Blessing for Volunteers

O God of endless goodness,
day after day, we feast in your garden
among friends and family.

Thank You for those people
who give of themselves so freely.
Those who create a gentle and beautiful
web around us . . .
A community that corrects and challenges,
loves and encourages.
A community filled with volunteers
who build a home in a far-off corner,
who repair a sagging porch,
who bake pies,
who teach children to cut and paste,
who rake leaves for a neighbor,
and who sort books for the library sale.

For people who nurture life far away
and close to home,
hear our thanks.
May the witness of those who give
muscle, mind, and money
mold us so that reaching deeply
becomes a pattern of our lives as well.

Blessing for the Friend Who Brings Dinner

God of Sustenance,
for nourishment that comes
homemade and from the heart,
my body and soul are full.

This gift is not "just" anything.
If the ingredients had been gathered
fresh from a farm that morning,
the taste could not be sweeter.

I savor a second helping straight from the dish . . .
A helping that is so good—
irresistibly good,
like this friendship.

May the taste of this blessed moment
feed me today—
and nourish my words and actions
in the days to come.

Blessing for the Mammogram Technician

Bless You, God of Nurture,
for my yearly doctor's visit.
For this person whose work
requires such precision and skill
in the face of many challenges,
bodies of all shapes and sizes . . .
Bless this technician who offers
a beautiful and critical gift:
the opportunity to protect and understand
the body that has long sustained me.
I could never fully express my thanks.

As the machine presses down on me,
I am grateful to be at this altar of life.

Blessed are You, God of Nurture,
for this sacrament,
pure and simple,
and for those who bestow it.

Blessing for the Realtor, Saleswoman, Accountant, and Other Guides

God who goes before us,
a cloud by day,
a pillar of fire by night,
You're not always showy,
but You're always present in our lives.

Bless the simple guides who show up
and are, in the moment, more helpful
than we could ever hope or imagine:
The realtor who appears
with carpet samples and paint chips.
The saleswoman at the department store
who helps us pick the best color
when we can't decide.
The accountant who prepares our taxes,
the bottom line less painful
when it comes from his calculator.

Bless their wisdom and guidance,
so sweet, simple, and holy.
The trying tasks feeling somehow lighter
when we follow the lead of another.

Blessing for a New Adventure

Generous One,
You are the mystery and wonder
at the heart of life.
If You had just formed us
from Your breath and dirt
and put us in the garden
to love and to eat,
it would have been enough.

But You called us
to till and to keep Your creation, too.
You invited us to share in Your creative work.
This day look with favor
upon the world that You have
made and redeemed.
And look with favor
upon those of us setting out
to do something new.

Benediction for a Gathering of Loved Ones

We say our farewells
with this holy prayer . . .
The Lord bless you and keep you;
the Lord's face smile upon you,
and be gracious to you;
the Lord's presence turn toward you,
and give you peace.

BASED ON NUMBERS 6:24-26

Blessings for the Places I Go

We were in Botswana, in southern Africa. David, our friend and guide, had pulled the truck over and pointed to a pile of white rocks, large and mound-like, by the side of the road. "That's a sign of healing. People have marked this place on a trip to say it is sacred. *Holy.*"

I thought of his words again later in Lesotho, as we placed rocks on the grave of his daughter. *Sacred.*

We mark certain places with rocks—sometimes literally, but more often with our minds. We think of places where we have been changed, moved, lost, healed, or transformed, and we feel their holiness.

When I was a kid, my best friends and I spent hours playing in the creek behind my house. We'd jump from rock to rock. We'd catch crawdads with bacon strips, string, and a coffee can. For us, the creek was a holy place.

The more we mark certain places as holy, set apart, the more we begin to note how all the world is sacred, set apart. Rocks by the road remind us. So does a rope swing over a creek, a marker in the family graveyard, or a yellow ribbon around a tree. Every inch of the earth is filled with the holy, saturated with God's presence, and alive with potential for healing and discovery.

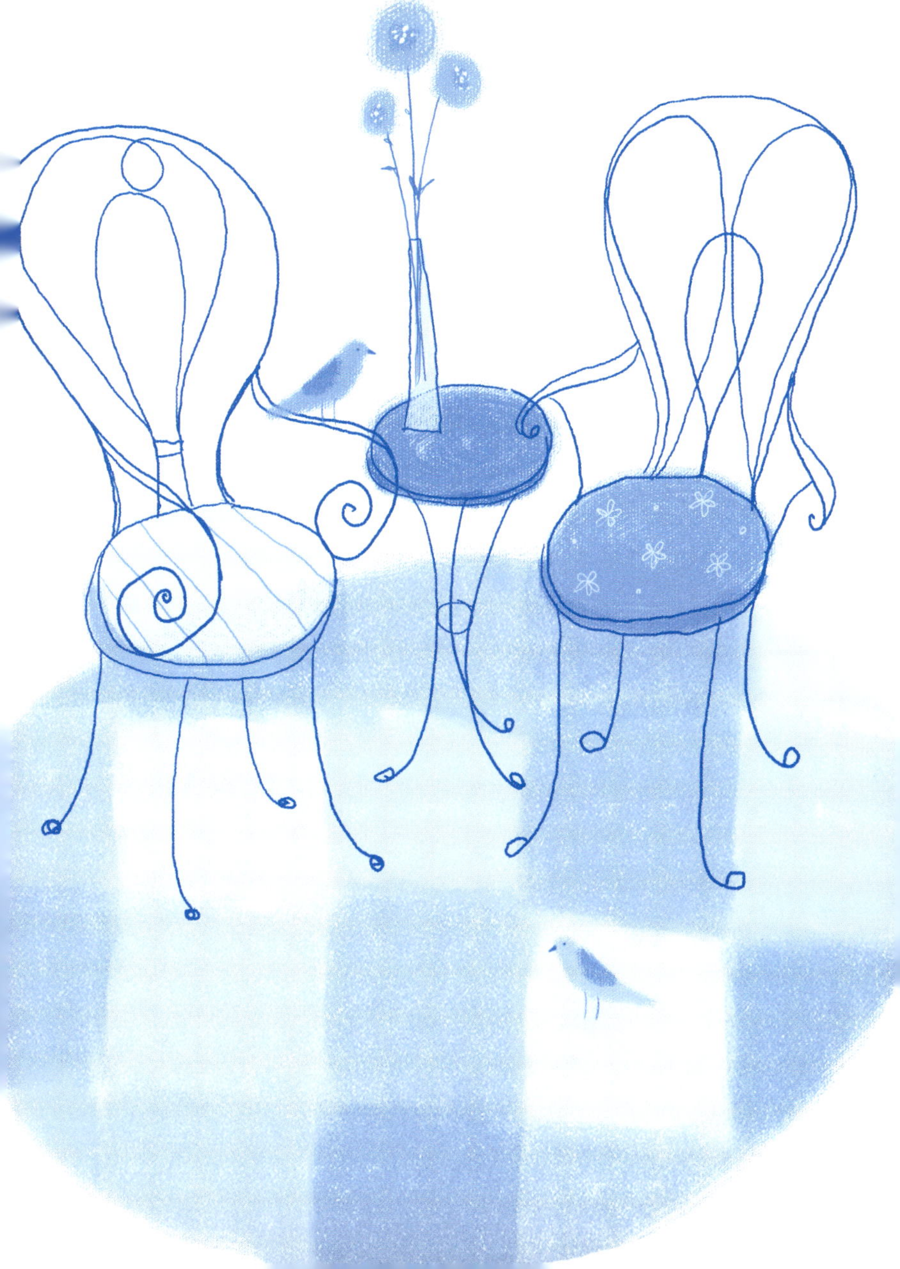

Blessing for My Home

What can I say, Holy One,
that You have made a home for me?

You have made the earth.
From the highest heavens where
the moon and stars compete for center stage
and the space shuttle soars,
to the ocean depths
where corals and fish of every color
coexist beneath the reach of sunlight.

You have made our own little worlds, too—
the breakfast table
where we get moving, up and out the door,
and the evening bed where
we lay before our bodies drift off to sleep . . .
You are there always
in any place we dwell.

Bless my home.
Bless these four holy walls
that within their sanctuary,
I might feel Your presence ever and always.

Blessing for My Job

Holy One,
You call me to live boldly—
and I receive that call as the gift it is,
a gift that is mystery and miracle,
discipline and devotion.

You call me to till soil
and build mountains,
creating and giving as I also take and receive.
You ask that I understand Your gifts to me . . .
while I use those gifts to make my own offering
to You and Your world.

I give thanks now for the gift of work,
for thinking up new ways to fix a problem,
for the chance to be part and parcel of creation,
for the grace of serving and then feasting
on my labors.

God, for my skills that are valued, needed,
and helpful to others,
hear my thanks.

Blessing for a Friend's House

Bless my friend's house,
the comforting feel of the couch,
the carpet with its fibers knit together
like our years of friendship.

Bless this holy, nurturing, life-giving home.
Bless this refuge for my tears
and headquarters for my soul.

For toasting the best moments,
saying grace,
and serving the feast,
it is a sacred space.

Bless this house
and the delight and safety
I feel within.

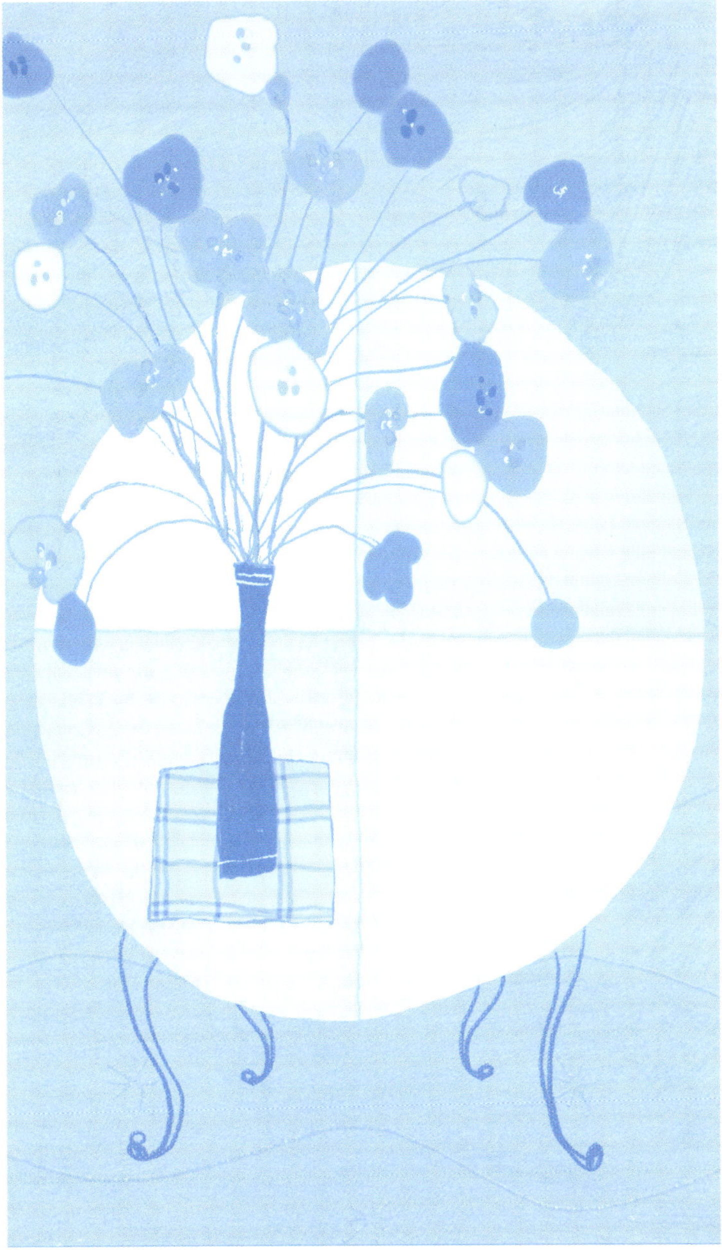

Blessing for Our Church

Hear our thanks, You Who Call Us,
for this holy place—
a sacred home where our deepest dreams
and wildest longings are given voice.
An inspirational home where mystery meets muscle
in service to Your creation.

In this space, our ties to one another
take shape and flesh.
Care becomes a phone call.
Concern becomes a pot of soup.
A new baby is kissed and passed.
The bitter and unspeakable are
shouldered and shared.

May these walls formed of wisdom and worship
ground us, gird us, and guide us
that we might be present to the needs
of the frail, the poor, the young, the old . . .
and that we might be quick to share
Your bounty and Your blessing.

Hear our thanks, Dear One,
for this sacred place,
where we come not to shut out Your world
but to attend more wisely to it.

Blessing for the Farmer's Market

God of All that is Ripe and Plentiful,
thank You for Your Garden.
The awesomeness of the market is overwhelming:
so many gifts all in one place,
offered for locals and weary travelers alike.

Bountiful One,
You come to us in the scent of flowers
fresh from the fields,
in the bite of a perfectly ripe berry,
or a sweet carrot straight from the farm.
In this manna from heaven
spread before us like a banquet,
we taste the deliciousness of life.

You are too much, Good God.
In the end, we will carry our small bounties,
still wishing we had more room
for all that You offer.

Blessing for the Checkout Line

God, whose timing
does not line up with mine
as I stand waiting,
let me not tap my toes impatiently.
Let me not stare wistfully
at the shorter line beside me
or the lane that inexplicably moves
faster than mine.

Instead, let me take this chance
to notice what I normally would not.
Open my eyes to the people around me,
these tender souls making purchases
to stock their lives and homes.
Whether we pay in credit, checks, cash,
or food stamps,
we come all to supply our needs—
each of us as Your beloved child.

Let me slow down so that
for a moment, God,
Your timing becomes mine.

Blessing for the Grocery Store

Bless this place, Holy God,
where we find so much bounty:
the aisles neat and organized,
the order and patterns of color,
the progression from cold
to room temperature to cold again.
Bless the nourishment:
grapes, green beans, avocadoes, and apples.

Here we are reminded that Your abundance
can never be exhausted.
Your deliveries come daily, without fail.
Food comes from the earth to a truck
to a shelf to a cupboard—
touched by hands every step of the way.
Bless those hands—
especially those too young or too old
to be picking or those too lowly to be paid.
Nourished by Your food,
may we be the change we wish to see,
a force for justice and grace in Your world.

Blessed are You, God of Plenty and Delight.

Blessing for a World Needing Peace

God of Peace, we come to You
in a world that so often lacks for peace.
We see it, painfully, in ourselves—
the sharp words that come so fast,
the pits, cavern-like in our souls,
when we feel threatened or afraid.
The whirl that keeps us running
from our calendars to our cars.

The morning papers bring news of riots
in distant lands, killings on a campus,
and companies committed to the bottom line
instead of to the people stuck on the bottom.

Slow me, somehow, with the blanket of night
or with a morning frost on my window.
Give me the dedication I need to face my demons
and the hope I need to face hostility, straight on.

In a world that so often lacks for it,
let there be peace.
And let me be a force for it.

Blessing for Leaving a Place

You send me out, Dear One, whistling,
my step a bit lighter,
my vision brighter,
confident that the earth is a gracious place,
ready to receive and embrace me.

I see Your horizon stretching out before me,
and it is wide open.
I step out, feeling thankful, open, expectant,
and ready to move into the arms
of Your beautiful world.

Blessings for the One and Only Me

When my firstborn was tiny, a small boutique store had a beautiful coat in the store window: a rich red wool with a full skirt and a black velvet collar. The deepest red and the softest velvet—elegant, simple, graceful. It reminded me of Caroline Kennedy standing quietly in the cold as her father's casket passed by. It was a coat for a child who was treasured and adored.

I had a coat like that once, a cape of blue velvet. My mother, my favorite shopping companion, pointed to the red coat now and asked, "Do you remember your sweet velvet cape?" I had not thought about it in years, but in the blink of an eye, I could see myself: a little girl, blonde hair, pixie cut, white tights, black patent leather shoes, and the blue velvet cape.

"I have it, now, for Eden," my mother told me. "Aunt Mary replaced the old lining with a blue silk."

So the blue cape came back to me—a treasure that told me I was royal and cherished. A family treasure, passed down and handed on. It was like the story of Jesus' baptism—when the heavens open and Jesus hears a voice saying, "You are my beloved, in You I am well pleased." The early Christians passed that story down, like a precious cape, so the young would know: You are chosen, and you are blessed.

May the blessings in this book be a royal cape for your shoulders. May they mark you as the holy, gifted, priceless being that you are.

Prayer of St. Francis

Gracious God,
make me an instrument of your peace.
Where there is hatred, let me sow love.
Where there is injury, pardon.
Where there is doubt, faith.
Where there is despair, hope.
Where there is darkness, light.
Where there is sadness, joy.

O Divine Master,
grant that I may not so much
seek to be consoled, as to console;
to be understood, as to understand;
to be loved, as to love.
For it is in giving that we receive.
It is in pardoning that we are pardoned,
and it is in dying that we
are born to Eternal Life.

Blessing for Using My Unique Gifts

God who called Abraham and Sarah,
Martin and Rosa,
in every age You call
Your sons and daughters
to serve.

You call me to use my unique gifts
for my unique purpose,
to live out not another's call—
because that would be a poor imitation.
You ask me to live out of my center,
to acknowledge You as the beat of my heart,
the breath in my lungs.
Give me the strength to use the gifts
You've given me, God,
to understand that I am a work
of Your creative genius.

Blessing for Life's Abundance

Dear One,
if You had only made the prairies
with wheat waving in the wind,
rich ears of corn stretching to the sky—
and You'd left out the tall pines
and Rocky Mountains—
it would have been enough.

If You had only given us the clear creeks,
water lapping and sparkling,
trickling over rocks,
and You'd left out the oceans
with crashing waves and sandy beaches,
it would have been enough.

If You had only made us in Your image,
put us in the garden to till and to keep,
filled our hours with meaningful work—
and You'd left out the Sabbath
to relax and play—
it would have been enough.

If You had only given us mothers, fathers,
sisters, and brothers—
and You'd left out soul mates, best friends,
and trusted colleagues—
it would have been enough.

But Your nature is love.
Abundant, overwhelming, unsurpassable.
Day in and day out,
we receive at Your hand
what we have neither created nor earned.
Bless You, Dear One,
for loving us so much more than enough.

Blessing for a Relationship With God

You're known by many names:
Creator, Healer, Redeemer, and more. . .
words that attempt to give shape to Your love.

Hold me close as I stand before You:
working, but sometimes struggling
to imitate Your model of love,
learning, growing, and transforming
all the days of my life.

Hold me close as I hold Your light
up to the places where I need
maturity and development:
the rough edges of my personality,
the reactionary way I may handle anger and hurt,
the quick way I accuse,
or the slow way I forgive.

Hold me close as I bring before You those I love:
children growing up in a world spinning fast,
brothers with issues and sisters in distress,
coworkers and friends whose paths
are anything but smooth.

Hold this world tenderly, from Kansas to Kandahar.
May the mystery of Your care draw us all closer,
Creator, Healer, Redeemer . . .
May these words shape my life—
and my relationship with You.

Blessing for the One and Only Me

Dear One, You called this world into being.
The earth, sea, and sky are Yours.
Every atom is full of Your energy.
There is no place I could go to escape Your mercy.
No crack, crevice, or closet You would not search,
turn inside out,
scour and sweep
to find me.

No matter how deep the mine
into which I have fallen
or how many covers I have pulled over my head,
still, You draw me to You.
You enfold me, surround me,
enter my speaking and my thinking.
You come into my life and out of my lips,
into my soul and out of my skin.

Ever-present God,
turn my gratitude into graciousness,
my uncertainty into assurance,
and my hopes into purpose,
so that I, as singular as I am,
might be as fully present to my life as You are.

Blessing for Rest and Relaxation

God of the Sabbath Rest
and Much-Needed-Breaks,
You spread Your gifts before us.

You invite us to breathe in the early morning quiet,
before the world wakes and noise floods our lives.
You invite us to breathe in the afternoon,
curled up with a good book or a walk with a friend.

You give us an evening all alone
or a weekend with Saturday-morning chores
completed and checked off.

The spring break, the winter break,
the beach vacation,
the blessed change from the usual pace,
the time off with family and friends . . .

For rest and the much-needed break
and for every gift that invites us deeper in to You,
hear our thanks.

Blessing for Generous Living

Dear One, because the world is
beautiful and fragile,
and because You have called me
to be Your steward,
I need Your help.
For I know that my tenderness
can be threatened by my harshness—
and that You call me to live generously.

I need Your strength and compassion
in this world, where lives can be swept away
in an instant by a wave of water.
In this world where lives can be eroded
over time, by indifference.

I need Your guidance because You have
created me for service.
Help me see that the things I have
should contribute to the good of others—
and that the things I do not have
are of no central concern.

Sweet Spirit of Life,
may the gifts I have—
my hopes and dreams,
my longings and loves,
become Your faith and Your food on earth.

Blessing to Hear God's Call

God, I'm listening for Your call today—
Your voice new and fresh.
More than a crash where the heavens split
and Your voice is shouted above the wind . . .
More than an appointment reminder
left on voice mail . . .
I'm listening for Your persistent, insistent call.

Amazing God, You never give up.
You're in tireless pursuit of my heart.
You hit redial over and over until I pick up.
Not once or twice,
but a thousand times a thousand.
Even when I am bone-weary and unsure,
You are there.
You persist until all parts of me—
loves and longings, marbles and treasures,
are laid on the table for You to see and to sort.

Bless You for Your call
to receive and to share.

Blessing for My Recovery

God of setbacks and of sickness,
thankfully, I fell.
And even more thankfully,
I stumbled on a path to recovery.
Slow and tedious,
I come to a place on the path
I would not have chosen for myself.
Not ever.
Now I stop to stretch,
working the routine
to build muscle, tone, and a flexible spirit.
I stop to appreciate
all that I took for granted before.

God who created me helpless—
dependent for my very life . . .
Could I have guessed I'd need such care?
Bless the ones who have held me,
fed me, and soothed me.
May this downtime,
this healing time,
rebuild my body and my being.

Blessing for My Hands

Holy One,
these hands have made mud pies
and finger paintings,
cut an apple and brushed a dog,
held a hand and rubbed a back,
planted seeds and weeded gardens,
written a lover and a legislator . . .

Holy One,
may these hands
show the sign of Your guiding hand,
Your steadfast presence.
May their work
be always Your holy work.

Blessing for My Limitations

Great Heart,
Your beauty and power,
grace and mercy are without limit.

I know too well my own limits.
I can't keep up with the job and the housework.
I can't keep the family happy and the car running.
I can't stay up with the news—
not even the front-page story.

In my very real limits,
comfort me with this awareness:
You are God.
Not I.
Grant me peace, knowing that
You have created the world.
Not I.
Help me remember that You can re-create
that which I damage.

Open me to the power of Your love,
which is without limit.
Open me to Your peace,
which passes understanding.
Open me to Your strength and spirit
until I find that my limits no longer limit me.

Blessing for All of Who I Am

Searching One,
You see all of who I am:
the good and bad,
the patient and pushy,
the generous and hoarding.

You see the warm heart embracing.
And You see the cold heart pushing away.

You love me apart from what I am
and what I am not,
apart from what I've done
and what I've not done.

You see all of who I am,
and still You claim me
and name me as Your own.

Help me to see myself as You do.
The potential.
The off-the-charts possibilities
that can lift me
beyond any limit.

If you have enjoyed this book
or it has touched your life in some way,
we would love to hear from you.

Please send your comments to:
Hallmark Book Feedback
P.O. Box 419034
Mail Drop 215
Kansas City, MO 64141

Or e-mail us at:
booknotes@hallmark.com